Our Changing World

THE TIMELINE LIBRARY

THE HISTORY OF THE AUTOMOBILE

BY KEVIN CUNNINGHAM

1850   1900   1950   2000   2050

THE CHILD'S WORLD® • CHANHASSEN, MINNESOTA

Published in the United States of America by The Child's World®
PO Box 326 • Chanhassen, MN 55317-0326 • 800-599-READ • www.childsworld.com

ACKNOWLEDGMENTS

The Child's World®: Mary Berendes, Publishing Director

Editorial Directions, Inc.: E. Russell Primm, Editorial Director; Katie Marsico, Associate Editor and Line Editor; Judith Shiffer, Assistant Editor; Matt Messbarger, Editorial Assistant; Susan Hindman, Copy Editor; Sarah E. De Capua, Proofreader; Peter Garnham, Olivia Nellums, Molly Symmonds, and Stephen Carl Wender, Fact Checkers; Tim Griffin/IndexServ, Indexer; Cian Loughlin O'Day, Photo Researcher; Linda S. Koutris, Photo Selector

The Design Lab: Kathleen Petelinsek, Design and Art Production

Content Adviser: Roger B. White, Curator, Smithsonian Institution, Washington, D.C.

PHOTOS

Cover/frontispiece images: Bettmann/Corbis (main); Library of Congress (left inset); Toyota/Lexus (right inset).

Interior: Bettmann/Corbis: 7, 13, 21; Corbis: 5 (Austrian Archives), 10, 24 (Matthew Mcvay), 26 (Sandy Felsenthal); Getty Images/Hulton|Archive: 9, 17; Getty Images/Scott Halleran: 29; Getty Images/Time Life Pictures: 14 (Joseph Scherschel), 18 (J. R. Eyerman), 23 (Bill Pierce).

Timeline: Bettmann Corbis: 16, 20, 21, 23; Corbis: 25 (Jim Sugar); 27 (Henry Horenstein); Getty Images/Fotos International: 28; The Granger Collection: 6; Library of Congress: 8, 10; Library of Congress/Detroit Publishing Company: 12, 15; NASA/Kennedy Space Center: 22; Pictures Now: 18.

LIBRARY OF CONGRESS CATALOGING-IN-PUBLICATION DATA

Cunningham, Kevin (Kevin H.)
  The history of the automobile / by Kevin Cunningham.
    p. cm. — (The timeline library (series))
  Includes index.
  ISBN 1-59296-343-9 (library bound : alk. paper) 1. Automobiles—History—Juvenile literature. I. Title. II. Series.
  TL147.C85 2004
  629.222'09—dc22   2004003738

TABLE OF CONTENTS

CATCHING A RIDE

Kaya had a busy day ahead of her. She had to get to school, and later that afternoon her softball team was playing a championship game in a neighboring town. Afterward, Kaya and her family were going to a local restaurant for pizza. It was important that Kaya get to these places on time, and walking would take forever!

"Do any of your friends need me to drive them to the game, Kaya?" her father asked as he pulled his car into the school parking lot.

"I'll ask them," said Kaya. "Thanks for the ride, Dad!" Kaya waved good-bye to him as he drove away. The day was going to be filled with activity, but having a car would make getting where she needed to go much easier.

In the late 1800s, engineers, inventors, and tinkerers worked to create the automobile. At first, driving was considered an expensive hobby, but the car

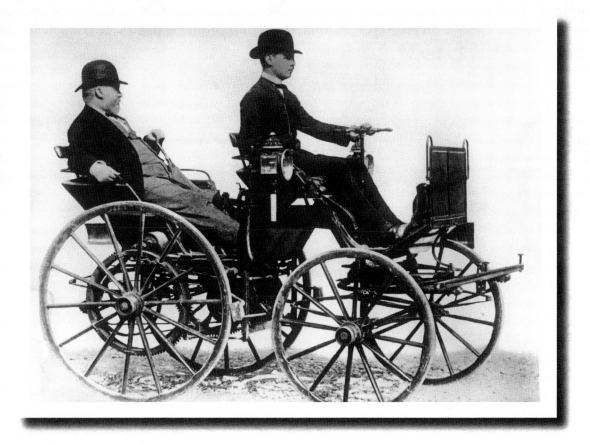

From 19th-century motorcars such as the one shown here, to the sporty, speedy vehicles of the 21st century, automobiles are one of our most important means of transportation.

was popular from the start. As the 19th century turned into the 20th, progress raced ahead. You couldn't keep up on horseback. Forget walking or bicycles. You needed wheels, a full tank of gas, and a lot of **horsepower.**

CHAPTER ONE

THE EARLY DAYS

German inventor Karl Benz got into the engine business to make money. He ended up making history. Benz spent much of his time working on an engine-powered vehicle. By early 1886, he received a **patent** for his latest invention, a noisy three-wheeler that ran on gasoline.

In 1888, Benz's updated version turned heads. "The amazement of everyone on the street . . . was such that they seemed unable to grasp what they had before their eyes," wrote one reporter. Benz soon made four-wheeled cars to sell. And sell they did, for a little while. Unfortunately, Benz refused to change the look of his carriagelike vehicles. The car was a new technology, but drivers already cared about style. Other automakers began capturing the car-buying audience and passed Benz by.

1886

Karl Benz receives a patent for his first three-wheeled vehicle (right).

Georges Seurat shows his painting *Sunday Afternoon on the Island of La Grande Jette.*

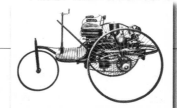

Charles Duryea, a bicycle maker from Peoria, Illinois, read about Benz's car and decided to build one of his own. He and his brother Frank secretly created a **prototype** in Springfield, Massachusetts. The car's first journey carried the smoking, sputtering machine 200 feet (61 meters).

Frank continued to work on his car and finally won a Chicago road rally in 1895. A year later, the brothers used the

Frank Duryea (right) won an Illinois road rally in 1895. During the race, Duryea traveled between Chicago and Evanston, a suburb just to the north.

1895

Frank Duryea wins a road rally in Chicago and becomes famous.

German scientist Wilhelm Röntgen discovers X-rays.

prize money to form the Duryea Motor Wagon Company. The Duryea factory produced 13 vehicles. But the Duryea brothers fought, and the company never took off.

1904: CARS FOR ORDINARY PEOPLE

Ransom E. Olds, a mechanic from Geneva, Ohio, had an incredible new idea—make cars to sell to ordinary people, instead of just to the rich. When a 1901 fire destroyed his workshop, he rescued only one of his 11 prototypes. But the automobile he saved was the Oldsmobile Runabout.

Olds attracted attention to the Runabout with cross-country drives and big promises. In 1904, more than 5,000 Runabouts rolled out the doors. It became the first big-selling car.

1901

Ransom E. Olds rescues his Runabout prototype from a fire.

An assassin shoots President William McKinley (right) on September 6.

Meanwhile, the Detroit Automobile Company was developing a future classic called the Cadillac. It used a new motor made by engineer Henry Leland. To show the motor's improved power, Leland told one of his staff to drive a Cadillac up the steps of a courthouse. The stunt helped make the car a hit.

Within a decade, people were able to drive to places far from the railway lines. Fewer and

1904

Olds sells more than 5,000 of the Oldsmobile Runabout.

New York City's first subway line begins operation.

Three ladies enjoy a ride in a Cadillac in 1901.

This 1902 race drew cheering crowds along Long Island Motor Parkway.

fewer horses clogged—and stank up—New York City's streets. Farmers living in rural areas could get to town to shop, attend church, or see friends. As early as 1902, racers roared past thousands of fans on Long Island and Daytona Beach.

A Michigan engineer saw the car taking over. "When I'm through," Henry Ford said, "everyone will be able to afford one, and just about everyone will have one. The automobile will be taken for granted." He was right.

1905

Theodore Roosevelt (right) begins his second term as U.S. president.

CHAPTER TWO

FORD AND THE MODEL T

Henry Ford hated farm work so he apprenticed himself to a mechanic at the age of 16. In 1896, Ford finished his first car. After working for Thomas Edison and the Detroit Automobile Company, Ford struck out on his own. He designed successful race cars and used the money he made to start the Ford Motor Company in 1903.

During its first year, the Ford Motor Company sold more than $1 million in cars. One of its racing cars, the 999, set a new land speed record. Barney Oldfield, driving without a clutch or seat belt, took the 999 up to 91 miles (147 kilometers) per hour on a frozen lake in Detroit.

But Ford's most famous product was the Model T in 1908. Ford set the starting price for the car at $825. It handled rough roads. Anyone with a

1908	Henry Ford introduces the Model T.

"Take Me Out to the Ball Game" is
the most popular song of the year.

THE MOVING ASSEMBLY LINE AT FORD'S HIGHLAND PARK FACTORY CHANGED BUSINESS FOREVER. FORD'S GOAL WAS TO PRODUCE A GREATER NUMBER OF CARS AT A CHEAPER COST.

EACH WORKER ON THE ASSEMBLY LINE PERFORMED A SINGLE TASK, SUCH AS PLACING PARTS ON A PIECE OF THE CAR AS IT WENT BY ON A CONVEYOR BELT. THE MOVING ASSEMBLY LINE REVOLUTIONIZED CAR MANUFACTURING BECAUSE MILLIONS OF CARS COULD BE PRODUCED AT A REDUCED COST. UNFORTUNATELY, THE WORK WAS DIFFICULT AND BORING, AND WORKERS QUIT CONSTANTLY.

few basic tools could do repairs. At first, it came in several colors, but not for long. Black paint dried faster which meant more cars could be churned out quicker. "You can have any color," went a famous saying, "as long as you want black."

By 1909, the Ford Motor Company had become the top U.S. auto company. Ford moved his operation into an enormous new factory in Highland Park, Michigan. In 1913, Ford had a moving assembly line installed in the factory that allowed cars to be made faster and cheaper. In 1914, he shocked everyone when he doubled his workers' wages to $5 a day. He could not afford to keep training too many new workers because that would slow down

1910 — Louis Chevrolet comes to the United States to design a new car.

Halley's Comet appears.

1913 — Ford improves the assembly line at his factory in Highland Park, Michigan.

Woodrow Wilson (right) becomes president.

production. Around the same time, the Model T's price dropped to $440 and soon to less than $300. Amazingly, Ford made more money than ever. This was partially because his workers could afford new cars with their higher salaries. Like many Americans who could afford to buy a car, they chose the Model T. It had become an **icon**.

1920s–1945: FORD VERSUS GM

By the late 1920s, however, Ford ran into trouble. He had only one successful car. How would future Fords be able to measure up to the popularity of the Model T?

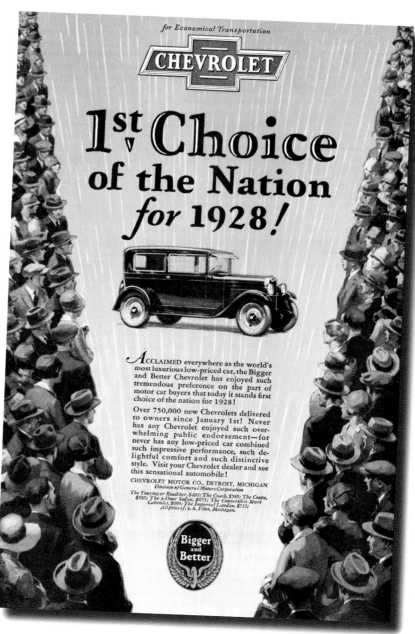

This advertisement from 1928 claimed that Chevrolet was America's first choice. The Chevrolet Motor Company was founded in 1911.

1914	Ford Motor Company doubles its workers' wages to $5 a day.
	Congress declares the first Mothers' Day.

Designer Harley Earl worked for GM from 1927 until his retirement in 1959.

Meanwhile, other car manufacturers such as General Motors (GM) and Packard borrowed Ford's methods of mass assembly. GM offered not one, but many different models such as the Cadillac, Chevrolet, and Pontiac.

While GM caught up, Ford's methods seemed increasingly outdated. GM, Chrysler, Packard, and others were selling the flashy cars people wanted in the 1920s. Ford stubbornly stuck to the Model T and basic black. Some

1921

Warren G. Harding becomes
the 29th U.S. president.

companies allowed people to use credit to buy a car. Ford hated credit.

Under designer Harley Earl, GM sold style. By 1927, the Model T's last year, GM threatened to leave Ford Motor Company in the dust. Ford attempted to sell more T's by finally offering it in bright colors, but to no avail. Eventually, the company introduced the Model A to compete with GM. That helped, but the Great Depression (1929–1939) soon cooled auto sales for all of the companies.

But after World War II, with jobs and money available, Americans again hungered for cars. New roads and a new way of life were just ahead. The automobile would be, in all ways, bigger than ever.

THE RISE OF NASCAR
BEFORE AND DURING THE GREAT DEPRESSION, EVERYDAY CARS BEGAN TO BE SOUPED UP FOR THE PURPOSE OF OUTRUNNING THE POLICE. THESE DRIVERS WERE OFTEN HAULING ILLEGAL LIQUOR. WILLIAM FRANCE DECIDED THAT SATURDAY NIGHT RACES BETWEEN THESE DRIVERS COULD BE POPULAR. HE FOUNDED THE NATIONAL ASSOCIATION FOR STOCK CAR AUTOMOBILE RACING (NASCAR) IN 1948. BY THE LATE 1960s, STOCK CARS CHANGED FROM BEING NORMAL ROAD CARS WITH POWERFUL ENGINES TO THE SUPER CARS OF TODAY.

1927

Ford makes the Model T for the last time.

Charles Lindbergh flies from New York to Paris.

CHAPTER THREE

ON THE ROAD

Cars made travel more convenient, but even the sturdy Model T was only as good as the roads it ran on. And in the early 1920s, roads remained bad. Most were old dirt paths for horses or carts. Rain turned them to mud.

In 1921, Congress passed the Federal-Aid Highway Act. Existing roads were repaired. New ones linking states were built. In 1925, a group of state highway officials assigned even numbers to east–west highways and odd numbers to north–south highways. That cleared up a lot of confusion.

1945–1965: A NEW CAR CULTURE

It was after World War II that America's car culture really took off. Auto shows attracted World Series–sized crowds, all wanting to see the latest models. At the

1921

Congress passes the Federal-Aid Highway Act.

Albert Einstein (right) wins the Nobel Prize in Physics.

same time, the United States entered the **Cold War.** The government began the interstate highway system both to connect the country and to potentially transport military equipment.

As it turned out, everyday drivers used the roads more than tanks or jeeps. Families piled into big steel cars or handy station wagons. Buyers in the 1950s had their choice of fantastic machines. GM put out the Corvette, an American sports car inspired by sleek European models. Both celebrities and average citizens lined up for Ford's sharp new Thunderbird. People drove everywhere, and they wanted to look good doing it.

New kinds of businesses sprang up to serve drivers.

This XP-700 Corvette was a popular new model in 1958.

1925

State highway officials assign even numbers to east-west highways and odd numbers to north-south highways.

Nellie Tayloe Ross becomes governor of Wyoming and the first woman governor in the United States.

Filling stations had been around almost as long as cars, selling gas, and motor oil, and maybe a refreshing, cold soda. Now architects created modern buildings with ever-brighter colors and bigger signs to attract drivers. Motels opened along the highways catering to people on road trips.

Food became fast food. Restaurant chains with gaudy signs promised dinner in a bag that could be served in minutes. You could watch movies from your car at the drive-in or park at a hamburger joint and get waited on by a girl on roller skates. Banks opened drive-through windows.

And just as it seemed cars could not get any larger, many Americans began turning away from big tail fins.

Two small cars made a splash in 1958. More than

1938

The Volkswagen Beetle first appears in Nazi Germany.

U.S. employers establish the 40-hour work week.

Drive-in movie theatres such as the one shown here became popular in the 1950s.

200,000 of American Motors' small, gas-saving Ramblers sold that year. The Volkswagen (VW) Beetle was an even bigger surprise. The Beetle first appeared in Nazi Germany in 1938. Noisy, plain-looking, and with an engine in the rear, the VW didn't cost much. Using humorous ads, VW targeted buyers turned off by the oversized, gas-hungry cars cranked out by American companies. Many sneered, but VW sold 10 million Beetles by 1965. It went on to be the best-selling car of all time.

The Big Three automakers—GM, Ford, and Chrysler—took notice. They began producing smaller cars. Their decision proved wise, as gas shortages, foreign cars, and new attitudes began to affect the auto industry.

1954

Ford's new Thunderbird (right) becomes an instant classic.

I Love Lucy is one of America's most popular TV shows.

1958

The AMC Rambler and VW Beetle become popular.

The United States launches its first satellite, *Explorer I*.

CHAPTER FOUR

1960–1980

T he Big Three tried to meet the needs of every buyer with a **diverse** fleet of station wagons, sports cars, small cars, and big luxury vehicles. However, one of the first attempts to meet and beat Europeans automakers was a disaster.

1964–1966: NEW MODELS AND A FOCUS ON SAFETY

GM's Chevrolet Corvair came with a daring European-style rear engine. The Corvair's design made it tricky to drive, but the car also came with a bad **suspension** system. Many accidents occurred.

In 1965, lawyer Ralph Nader wrote an **exposé** on unsafe cars such as the Corvair. His book, *Unsafe at Any Speed,* launched a movement to make cars safer. The National Traffic and Motor Vehicle Safety Act of 1966 forced automakers to

1964

Ford rolls out its popular Mustang (right).

One of the most powerful earthquakes in American history shakes southern Alaska.

install seat belts. Drivers started to consider safety features when choosing a car.

The success of small cars, however, overshadowed such mistakes. None succeeded like Ford's Mustang, which was released in 1964. With its long hood and short rear, the Mustang looked like a sports car but had a reasonable price. It was an unbelievable success. More than 1 million sold in less than two years. Soon a whole zoo of smaller cars, including Falcons and Sting Rays, filled the roads.

Car companies also answered the call for more power. Muscle cars came equipped with thirsty engines and lots of horsepower. They took off in 1964 when GM's Pontiac

In addition to being a lawyer and the author of Unsafe at Any Speed, *Ralph Nader is also a well-known politician.*

The book *Unsafe at Any Speed* is published.

Builders complete the Gateway Arch in Saint Louis (right).

Tempest Gran Turismo Omologato (GTO) Coupe appeared. Cars such as the Tempest and Chrysler's Cobra delivered nothing but speed and thrills—and speeding tickets.

Big cars hung on, too. The Oldsmobile Toronado appeared in 1965—more than 17 feet (5 m) of steel and luxury that sucked gas at a furious rate. The Cadillac Eldorado, with electric seat adjustment and one of the most powerful engines on the road, joined the Toronado in 1966.

1973–1980: FUEL-EFFICIENT CARS AND FOREIGN COMPETITION

Outside events soon changed the car industry again. In 1973, the Arab nations of Egypt and Syria attacked Israel. With help from the United States, the Israelis fought back.

1971

Apollo 15 (left) takes the LRV to the Moon.

Texas Instruments introduces the first pocket calculator.

The Arabs, angry at U.S. interference, announced an **embargo** on oil against the United States and its allies. For six months, Americans dealt with high prices, shortages, and frustrating lines at gas stations.

Drivers turned to small gas-saving cars. The Beetle, already fuel-efficient, continued to sell. But the Big Three did not make good **subcompact** cars. GM had to **recall** the disastrous Chevrolet Vega three times for safety reasons. Several Ford Pintos exploded—and several people died—when other vehicles hit them in the rear.

A fuel shortage in 1979 created long lines at gas pumps across the country and increased the popularity of fuel-efficient vehicles.

1973 The Arab-Israeli conflict leads to an oil embargo against the United States.

Artist Pablo Picasso (right) dies on April 8.

1978 Japanese automaker Honda introduces the Accord.

Louise Brown, the first test-tube baby, is born in Great Britain.

23

Japanese companies filled the need for safe subcompact cars. Though not much to look at, the Honda Accord and Toyota Corolla saved gas. Better yet, they rarely broke down. Americans bought them by the thousands.

The Big Three suffered. Ford lost more than $3 billion in three years. In 1980, the government had to save Chrysler from going broke. That year marked the first time that Japanese automakers ever made more cars than the Americans. U.S. factories closed, and workers lost their jobs. American companies were used to leading. Now they'd have to fight back from behind.

1980

The U.S. government loans money to Chrysler to save it from bankruptcy.

CNN goes on the air.

Japanese import cars await transport at a Seattle dock in the late 1980s.

CHAPTER FIVE

THE COMEBACK AND THE FUTURE

The Big Three automakers knew customers were unhappy. Recalls and repairs cost all three companies millions. Things got so bad Americans joked that the letters in Ford stood for "Fix or Repair Daily."

To make things worse, workers at these companies distrusted their leaders. Each side blamed the other for problems. Managers and workers cooperated in Japanese companies. The Japanese also proved excellent at getting the word out about their vehicles. Not only did customers buy their cars, they bought them year after year.

To save money, the Big Three cut their number of employees. The move devastated factory towns such as Flint, Michigan. Tens of thousands of people lost dependable, good-paying jobs. Even when things got better, **automation** and jobs

1980

Mount Saint Helens (right) erupts in Washington and kills 57 people.

Sparks fly at a Ford assembly plant in Chicago. The Ford Taurus is produced at plants such as the one shown here and continues to be America's best-selling car.

sent to other countries meant companies did not need all their old workers anymore.

1990s: CREATIVE STYLES AND CONCERN FOR THE ENVIRONMENT

Needing new ideas, Ford borrowed one from the Europeans: rounded corners. Some people laughed at these "bubble" or "jellybean" designs, but car buyers didn't. The "Euro-style" Ford Taurus eventually became the best-selling American car. Soon, old favorites such as the Lincoln and Thunderbird came out in sleek new styles.

Mistakes and economic problems hurt the Japanese

1987

NASCAR's Bill Elliott sets a record of more than 212 miles (341 km) per hour at the Talladega Superspeedway in Talladega, Alabama.

France and the United Kingdom agree to build a tunnel beneath the English Channel.

companies in the 1990s. Chrysler became a German company by joining Daimler-Benz A.G., maker of the Mercedes-Benz. GM bounced back with the Saturn. Built in a factory with Japanese-style cooperation between managers and workers, the Saturn became an affordable favorite. It is still one of the most popular choices for people buying their first car.

New concerns and buying habits have again changed what we see on the road. Small cars such as the BMW Mini Cooper and a new VW Beetle appeal to drivers worried about polluting the environment. At the other extreme, massive utility vehicles such as the Ford Explorer and Humvee are more popular—and guzzle more gas—than ever.

What about the cars of the future? Electric cars are

LICENSE PLATES
IN THE EARLY 1900S, STATES DECIDED TO MAKE THE OWNERS REGISTER THE VEHICLES. THAT ALLOWED STATES TO KEEP TRACK OF CARS AND TO RAISE MONEY FOR ROADS AND OTHER IMPROVEMENTS. OWNERS HUNG THE PLATES ON THE EAR AND SOMETIMES THE FRONT OF THEIR VEHICLES, DEPENDING ON WHERE THEY LIVED. BUT THERE WERE EXCEPTIONS. VERMONT, FOR INSTANCE, LET THE OWNER PAINT THE NUMBER ON THE CAR'S RADIATOR.

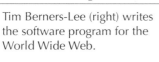

1990

The first Saturns go on sale.

Tim Berners-Lee (right) writes the software program for the World Wide Web.

here. In fact, battery-powered cars existed in the auto's earliest days. GM put one out in the 1990s, but drivers disliked that it needed to be "plugged in" so often. Still, some people think electric cars are the answer to problems such as global warming and dependence on foreign oil.

Hydrogen fuel cells are another idea. Currently, they cost a lot to make. They may require a whole new style of car, too. Inventors have had trouble making one powerful enough for a car, but they keep trying because they see many advantages. Fuel cells are clean, giving off water instead of chemicals. The cars would be silent. And there's far more hydrogen available than oil. GM says it has spent almost $1 billion on the cells already.

1998

Daimler-Benz A.G. buys Chrysler for $40 billion.

The film *Titanic* wins 11 Academy Awards.

Hybrid cars have already made an impact. The few available models, such as the Toyota Prius and Honda Insight, run on a combination of a gas engine and an electric battery. And more hybrids are in the works.

No one is sure which idea will win the race. But if car buyers go along with any of them, it will mean the biggest change in transportation since Henry Ford got people to give up their horses.

A standard Toyota Prius has a starting price of about $20,000.

2003 The space shuttle *Columbia* blows up over Texas, killing seven astronauts.

automation (aw-tuh-MAY-shuhn) Automation is the process of replacing human workers with mechanical ones. In the 1980s, many autoworkers lost their jobs because of automation.

Cold War (KOHLD WOR) The Cold War was a political and economic conflict between the Soviet Union and the United States that lasted from the mid-1940s until the late 1980s. The U.S. government created the interstate highway system in response to the Cold War.

diverse (duh-VURSS) Diverse means varied. GM competed with Ford by putting out a diverse group of cars.

embargo (em-BAR-goh) An embargo is a rule or law against selling a product or service. Arab nations used an embargo on oil to punish the United States for helping Israel.

exposé (ek-spoze-AYE) An exposé is a report, book, or article exposing wrongdoing. Ralph Nader's exposé on the Corvair led to new safety laws.

horsepower (HORSS-pou-ur) Horsepower is a way of measuring the pulling power in an engine or other machine. The fast muscle cars in the 1960s offered engines with a lot of horsepower.

hybrid (HYE-brid) A hybrid is something made up of two seemingly different kinds of parts. Cars in the future may have hybrid engines that use both gasoline and electricity.

icon (EYE-kon) An icon is an emblem or symbol, but it can also mean something that is worshipped or adored. The Model T became an icon in the early part of the 20th century.

patent (PAT-uhnt) A patent is a legal document giving an inventor of an item the sole rights to manufacture or sell the item. Karl Benz received a patent for his first three-wheeled vehicle in 1886.

prototype (PROH-tuh-tipe) In automaking, a prototype is a full-scale model used to test a new car design. Ransom E. Olds used his Runabout prototype to develop the first popular automobile.

recall (REE-kawl) A recall is a call by a company for the return of a bad or defective product. Many recalls of Ford cars hurt the company's reputation.

subcompact (sub-KOM-pakt) A subcompact is one of the smallest types of autos sold to the public. The Big Three automakers did not make good subcompact cars, but the Japanese did.

suspension (suh-SPEN-shuhn) A car's suspension is the system of springs and other devices supporting the upper part of the vehicle. GM covered up the Corvair's faulty suspension even though it led to accidents.

FOR FURTHER INFORMATION

AT THE LIBRARY

Nonfiction

* Bankston, John. *Henry Ford and the Assembly Line.* Bear, Del.: Mitchell Lane, 2004.

Burgan, Michael. *Henry Ford.* Milwaukee: Gareth Stevens, 2002.

* Georgano, Nick. *Beaulieu Encyclopedia of the Automobile.* Chicago: Fitzroy Dearborn, 2001.

Guttmacher, Peter. *Jeep.* New York: Crestwood House, 1994.

Temple, Bob. *Henry Ford: Automobile Manufacturer and Innovator.* Chanhassen, Minn.: The Child's World, 2003.

Weitzman, David. *Model T: How Henry Ford Built a Legend.* New York: Crown, 2002.

Fiction

Herman, Parish, and Lynn Sweat (illustrator). *Good Driving, Amelia Bedilia.* New York: Greenwillow Books, 1995.

* Books marked with a star are challenge reading material for those reading above grade level.

ON THE WEB

Visit our home page for lots of links about the automobile:
http://www.childsworld.com/links.html

Note to Parents, Teachers, and Librarians: We routinely check our Web links to make sure they're safe, active sites—so encourage your readers to check them out!

PLACES TO VISIT OR CONTACT

Henry Ford Museum
20900 Oakwood Blvd.
Dearborn, MI 48124-4088
313/982-6100

National Automobile Museum
10 Lake Street South
Reno, NV 89501
775/333-9300

Smithsonian National Museum of American History
14th Street and Constitution Avenue
Washington, DC 20560

ABOUT THE AUTHOR

KEVIN CUNNINGHAM IS AN AUTHOR AND TRAVEL WRITER WHO HAS
WRITTEN FOR NEWSPAPERS, MAGAZINES, AND TRAVEL GUIDES. HE
STUDIED HISTORY AND JOURNALISM AT THE UNIVERSITY OF ILLINOIS AT
URBANA. HE DRIVES A TOYOTA COROLLA, AND IN THE PAST HAS OWNED
MANY CARS, INCLUDING AN ENORMOUS 1977 PURPLE CADILLAC.